Flood Alert

For Wenna, Robbie, Laura and Michael

Flood Alert

Ian Crockatt

Chapman Publishing
1996

Published by
Chapman
4 Broughton Place
Edinburgh EH1 3RX
Scotland

A catalogue record for this volume is
available from the British Library.
ISBN 0-906772-79-6

Chapman New Writing Series
Editor Joy Hendry
ISSN 0953-5306

The publisher acknowledges the financial assistance
of the Scottish Arts Council.

Some of the poems and versions of the poems have
appeared in the following magazines and anthologies:

*Southern Arts, Workshop New Poetry, The Rialto, Iron, Chapman,
Northwords, The Broken Fiddle, Poetry Book Society Supplements,
Poetry Dimension Annual 3* (Robson Books), *Over to You* (English
Speaking Board), *Hidden Talent – The Workshop Poets* (Russel Hill
Press), and *New Writing Scotland*.

A few of these poems were originally collected in an Outposts
Publications booklet called *On Each White Page*.

Cover design: Fred Crayk
Author's photograph: Bodie's Photographic Services

Printed by
Econoprint
112 Salamander Street
Leith

Contents

Introduction

Ian Crockatt's working landscape is a varied one. He was born in Perth, schooled chiefly in England, lives near Fort William and works in Banff. Yet, his *poetic* landscape is even more varied. For two decades, it has ranged over the widest geography of human concerns and emotions. A Crockatt poem is both intense and emotionally compact. He takes on any subject, leaving a well-wrought (often, *perfect*) poem which nevertheless must withstand scrutiny from his own sharp West Coast sailor's eye.

Presently, both Ian and I work in Banffshire. Through a series of informal gatherings under the rubric "The Hovel Poets", I have got to know his poetry even better and I have learned a lot from him about the complex art of poetry. His deep concern for people is matched by an uncanny, unerring insight into the technique of poetry, *without* sacrificing its emotional impact. Few good poets ever achieve that fine balance and bad poets never do, but Ian Crockatt achieves it consistently.

By his own admission, Ian Crockatt has never been a prolific poet (the price of perfection?) so this collection is all the more valuable for gathering together the work of this "poet's poet". Two decades late perhaps, but well worth the wait.

Tom Bryan
Strathcanaird, September 1996

Chair

Twin-setted, jumpered,
like a fat slumped woman down the pub
it hulks
broad as its base;
block and tackle might heave it from its place.

God knows when it squatted there, we're new;
the room
is respectful, gives it space –
it hogs the floor;
I find myself hhesitating at the door.

It's outrageous
that this green-upholstered, yellow-bellied heap
of shabby bits and poor
design
has such presence. It has. It shatters mine.

Instinct
hollers "kick the stuffing out of it!"
Elephantine
urge – batter it all week
and I doubt if it would even creak.

Besides,
the whole, hunched, inscrutable bulk of it
literally reeks
of grave old age,
its leathered hide is wrinkled with knowledge...

It just exists;
ponderous as mud; a big baggage
full of dead matter.
Of course.
That's why I struggle with the brute in verse...

Twin-setted, jumpered,
like a fat, slumped woman down the pub,
it hulks
broad as its base;
block and tackle couldn't heave it from its place.

The Man

Day of the red-veined eyelid, the sun-dulled
snake. Heat hounded the earth, defined
the separateness of sand, the ineptness of flesh,
the shining motionless ocean's defeat. The man

stripped, spread his towel; dreamed an imperfect moon,
a face seeking shadow, a cool tear tracing its curve
of grief, till the blistering itch of his back
outshone it. He rose. A jet trailed its bandage

through the blue. Ran, split that glassy ocean
peered salt-eyed through the bubbling world plunged
to its cool-ribbed sandy bed till his lungs
burst back into being; then rose again,

floated. Noon's glare. Behind the deadpan beach
sandhills hunched under heat-halos; behind them a wood,
stock-still. O cooling waters. His bright heap
of clothes and rectangle of towel were tiny, beckoned.

Man's Hair

Perhaps because a diminutive ginger
pugilist called Fraser

filled our junior school
with bragging how he'd flung that blond Crockatt fool

flat on his back in the park, and pinned him there,
I'd always loathed red hair.

Let just one ginger curl show
and up the brat popped, eyes, fists, inches below

mine, but weasly, wiry, goading mine to fight;
And me, in hero's light,

having just blacked the eye
of Robertson, the minister's boy, smugly

winking round the crowd, grinning down at Fraser,
shrugging off my blazer.

It could have been any-
thing, green eyes, freckles, gap-teeth, or spots, but I

crawled off the ground, at that rat's pleasure – a loud
joke starting from the crowd

as satirist Fraser,
grinning, winking round, offered me my blazer –

hating red hair. Shout 'carrot head' and I'd split
my rib-cage yelling it,

fancy a red-head, No
matter how sleek her thighs or liquid her no,

and I was derisive, I'd laugh like a drain,
and back the blonde again.

That lasted 14 years...
The first days hinted, a week confirmed worst fears,

and one week more turned shock to admiration
when, presumably on

the manhood kick again,
rebel, in hero's light, I closed ranks with men

of daring, principle – and sprouted Man's hair.
Positively ginger...

Strange how that waking beard
shifted the years' perspective, in two weeks cleared

the way for a hireling memory to stand
downstage at last and

recall the blinding fact
that Fraser Refused to Fist-Fight, that the act

of pinning me down for 10 was technical
triumph, but amoral –

a neat bloodless poem.
How I straddled those beardless years, king of them

then, eye ripe for red-haired women – screw the past! –
confident this would last.

Then time conjured Frasers
from its hat that challenged with open razors...

John

(16, hostel for 'disturbed adolescents', 13th year in care)

John brags of braining cats
on alley walls, 'one whack
and they're dead.'
His hobby is astronomy,
he knows the constellations
like the tattoos on his arms,
has a tough time articulating space.
Life is a matter of growing bigger,
biggest of all are the dead

John says. He's small, but bovver-booted,
brash as his sense of humour,
he takes on an unequal world,
gropes the starry darkness in his head.
Each planet confirms him alien.
he grins – 'one whack
and they're dead!'

Green Pool

Skies are scattered
suns dissipated in
the green pool.

Lilies grow flat
out to save
their flowers.

Bubbles break up
bursting slime's
deep seal,

stone is plop
in a green
wink devoured.

When sticks poke
in to stir
that lidded eye

no airbound
frog glides up
to parley.

Still Life

Thirteen barge-hulls beached
on the Severn's south bank.
They list and rust
like scuttled sardine tins
in waves of petrifying mud.
Sky's bruised. Tide's out.
from the safe sea-wall
platoons of trippers watch
the plummeting sun
fret their sinking bones.
Winter has frozen spring.
They plough the earth,
stem to stern in the creaming mud,
cluttered with summer waste,
old cans, brown reeds.
Nothing progresses.
The trippers shiver and stamp.
There's hardly time to blink
night falls so fast.

Adam, Eve

For aeons they flung
on earth through space
mimicking angels.
not a wing
between them, or bird's voice,
but their vulnerable bellies
were ivory-white
as Judas's might

have been.
They were the youngest
of creatures,
pregnant with man,
tremulous first
of God's creators,
lovers, glad.
They had

angelic guts,
and angels'
inventive eyes,
they turned rot
and terror to apples
and Paradise.
And if it seems odd
to trump up God

and Satan,
to think to fly
perfect and sure
as swans in
a nursery sky,
figure a choicer
conceit than theirs,
a finer refractor of terror's stares,

than Paradise.
It all spilled out
of two brilliant embryos'
heads. All ages embrace

their defeat,
shall hear the horrendous
wail of their birth
into carrion earth

for ever.
For here were no angels
but man, sweet Judas;
and swans beating over
were apples
flinging through space,
that couldn't deceive
Adam, Eve.

Of a Rented Room

Noted through the window
of a rented room its double bed,
pictures, books, its easy chair.
Saw sun trapped on its wall, a shadow
looming, my own head
and shoulders silhouetted there.

Saw the woman by its door
who was crying. Black
trousers, sweater, hair,
grief abandoned to its floor.
Knew the ring, the flinching back,
the knuckles of despair.

Felt nothing I could do.
Opened the street-door
fumbling keys, lit a cigarette.
Found nothing I could do
but leave her crying on its floor.
Broke down in the kitchenette.

Of Exorcism

Shadows rise out of shadow.
My woman moans in her dreams
and darkness pricks up its ears –
hooves, thundering out of the void.

She moves her legs, she sighs.
Owl, stunning the moonlit hills
to snatch his prey, is hardly
more ecstatic then than I –

fierce muscle clamped round
her inviolate body
out-breaching, out-reaching,
out-riding the devil,

while under that oiled
relentless stallion thrust,
insensible, soft as petal,
she shrieks dark melodies...

If mind would allow
that moment's ecstasy
that carves a Buddha's face
and casts out appetite!

But sweat blackens our sheets;
hooves circle the hills outside;
and owl flaps back to roost
his demon unexorcised.

The Less Predictable Trees

Rope, at intervals knotted and strung up
in trees to swing and be swung on,
is fine as a toy. I swung, burned
my knees, wrists, palms on rope

and loathed it as a boy. I loathed more
crushingly the less predictable
trees it dangled from – yet still I'll
grinningly shin up ropes to wave

at you, yes tremblingly caper
in half-climbed trees, who then were
top-branch acrobats, making monkeys
of rope, and now need not be.

Roundabout

1 Bravado

All brats are bog-full of filth – it's a state
of mind, or a lack of mind more likely.
But no cauldron of toads beats a baby
for sheer Ugh! – they make a fetish of it.
To hear them bawling their nappies off at
bag-eyed parents in cafes and shops, or see
them bald as plums in swampy prams, clearly
good for nothing except noise and shit –
and yes they screech and ooze like that all night –
is to confirm that no monstrosity,
no embryonic bag of din and pee,
will ever warp the womb of my bed-mate.
Give me that cauldron, its toady brews
and smells any day, but birth – that's Bad News.

2 New Moon

The Moon starts up. She's taut with our miracle,
I'm silent – there's little to shout about,
we're old hands, we've read all the articles,
it's our second time round this roundabout.
We lie like this, wide-eyed, most nights, feeling
beneath us the same sheets and the same bed
the same house, garden, the same earth spinning
that last year mocked us with a son born dead.

Hope and fear prostrate our structured pride.
we're on our knees begging you Mother Earth
for this life – bury the hatchet that buried
us then, make this an ordinary birth.
Night digests our prayer. She breaks, I lie
too close to doubt to speak. The moon creaks by.

21

3 Like a Prayer

Your lungs lie wrinkled, unswollen by air,
but already I listen for crying.
Like a father I dream, imagining
my dreams will crowd your mind, all realised there.
Wanting to warn you I plot each mistake
of my own half-life, plan great lives for you;
already you and I have laughed lives through

together, and spun worlds in our wake...
I'd laugh at myself if I wasn't so scared –
O my half-child I want so much for you,
from you, that you might never give or take!
Be born – let your lungs swell and your cry declare
that sure, emphatic life inhabits you,
and live, in spite of me, for your own sake.

4 Stone-Talk

It's dead, forget it. Stripped down, shoved back in
the brain and lost, it can't hurt, forget it.
What's to remember? My love sick and swollen
with fear, half-hopes, a cracked dream – forget it.
So a world's collapsed – who cares? I'm hard, flint
on a dead world's crust, and anything goes –
and if some soft jerk mourns me or blinks a hint
of shock, so what? It's no skin off my nose.
Mother Earth! What a cruel cockteasing bitch
of a world it is, what a ragbag of taunts
and callousness, what a whore – oh it haunts
us all with failure and blood this whore... Bitch,
bitch of the pimping moon, curse, writhe about
and I won't crawl, I'm stone – you've ground me out.

5 Ways, Words

Buried in bed, in sheets buried, in bed –
O bed of loss, of lust, of love, unloose
sheets of love, burier of lust, of loss,
let love's ways, love's words, crowd this spinning head.

Till then blood no crying, no crying. World
of cauldrons, toads, of whores and quick spawnings,
let seed find ways, find words of forgetting,
seed's ways, seed's words, crowd where death has curled.

Eye-white moon coldly circles our dark nights
and O the lily-white worlds we create.
Let time teach ways, teach words of forgetting.

Black-eyed Earth spins indifferent as night,
O the life and the love, the crying, the hate.
Let grief learn ways, learn words of forgetting.

6 Bravado

Under Snow

Here lies a woman
who opened her heart
and found a foetus in it.
Her shroud of dark hair grows.

Here lies a woman
who pitched a tent for
her new dream to live in.
Dreams break camp and go.

Here lies a woman
who swallowed the moon
a pill of light to mend her.
Hope fed on its glow.

Here lies a woman
who opened her thighs
to the cold probes of science.
The scars still show.

Here lies a woman
beneath whose brow
anguish proved sterile as
dead earth under snow.

Here lies a woman,
womb full of whispers
and silence. Even
her fingernails grow.

Concert – Their Puppet's Contempt

Red – the most precise of colours
that dots and makes distinct
such grey-eared crowds is red –
next the pink of applauding flesh.

They wait – a thousand clappers –
in crimson stalls, for sound's
pure hand to finger and fist
the untongued bell of their heads.

Their brilliant puppet must
stoop, and stand, and then, then
shall his conjuring wand whisk
Tchaikovsky into the air – complete,

his riveting shout his miraculous
hair and – "Super, dear! Super!"
Fools. Back to them even, baton
poised, in command, I see red.

Finding the Place Again

Behind the broad beach are dumps
for nicotine-waste which are brown
as old blood and smell disgustingly –

like sores the dunes congeal round be-
tween broken pines and the sea where
gales gust so fast they stop you breathing.

This is where the sea destroys the land,
where nature devours herself, where salt
glazes your eyes like smoke and fouled

brown lungs are spread for all to see.
This is the place, this is where I played
out the dusk of my childhood days while

wagons came and went like rasping breath,
where meagre grasses stooped and under
their roots the whole world poured away.

Epitaph, with Quote

His song hatched
low in the last swan's throat
winged high and nowhere,

plunged paralysed
to the dark marsh grasses.
"*The very mountains*

loop stone arms round my neck."
A lather of feathers
and prickling terrors

is all he bequeathed;
and the blond moon
foundering in cloud.

Hitch-Hiking Home to Mother

Beside the croaking pond you sleep
sweet and rumpled on the garden lounger;
Sunday Times crisp at your feet,   ·
sycamore branches stooping over;
pale broad forehead specked with sweat,
ovened by freckled summer.

Indoors cool leisured shadows finger
the formal profile of your possessions,
long-fingered sleuths with moody questions
of paintings, clocks, plants, silver, mirrors,
the slightest most silent of inquisitions
staining your crimson-carpeted stair...

Ah, if England were not so tender,
if the yellowed teeth of the street
– the prosaic 'underprivileged' of your paper –
snapped, tore you blinking from sleep
while straight-backed sycamores quivered
and ponds closed over their deeps –

if England were not so tender...
I, hitching towards the brick-red sun,
the wealth I was born to – you, mother,
who waking chilled have deserted the lawn
for the draught-free ease of the sofa,
the chimeless clock's mahogany gleam

and the dazzle of magazine covers –
contemplate your bewildering cry,
my complicity in murder,
the breach and rape of luxury
the new massed fists of power,
the noose alive in the lightning-struck tree...

O mother you are earnest and sweet
as the rosy west that never says forever,
yet shadows darken your eyes. The fat
print trumpets our latest terrors
BOMB BLASTS OFF INNOCENT'S FOOT
OUT-OF-WORK MAN IS SHIRKER

RULES JUDGE, rule we, the privileged classes...
Mother this is my last trip home
to your kiss, the walled back lawn, the roses,
my first guerilla mission; the bomb
in my rucksack will scatter the multiple faces
of man O equally over the dim

astonished eye of God, and die.
forget me, close those deep red blinding curtains,
loving, anxious, sip your 9 o'clock tea;
tomorrow, at dawn, in your drumming garden,
the pond will brim with bloody rain
and choke the sycamore trees.

***

The last dark half-mile's hurry home
is punctuated by sniggers –
how noble, how gutless I've become.
For conscience beats a shallow drum,
and the heart booms angry, flows tender;
and I am your loving son, mother.

The Pressed Leaf

The leaf lay on the page,
sapless, flat,
killed not by age
but being picked and crushed; just that.

I touched the squashed veins
and splayed stem
which cool rain
had once made round and useful; and loved them,

and championed them in words,
wild – but look –
pressed, prematurely lifeless, hardly heard,
in a book.

A book which was a tree, minted
in pure rage,
now chopped, planked, pulped and printed;
page by page.

And I, on each white page,
sapless, flat,
crushed not by rage
but making words of it; just that.

Deaf and Dumb Love Song

The sea is a crumpled blanket –
only silence sails it,
every word we have ever said
has sunk through down
to its soundless bed, and broken.

Therefore our twittering hands
pretend to be songbirds,
all we have to say
takes off with the songbirds
to sing, and lands half-spoken.

I know the ear as
an empty concert hall
where nothing we have ever heard
is always about to be played,
I know silence as unbroken;

but I know there will be music
for your ears and mine,
know songs we cannot sing
will burst like a fist through glass,
and love will be spoken.

What Do Prophets Do on Bank Holidays?

(a refresher course on self-deception)

Jones leaves the vulgar city
– its winking neon glamour,
its ungodly barrage
of women and bills –

and craving new momentum,
some freshening mystery,
limps his grey way
to the darkening hills.

There night lays down its cloak
for Jones to kneel on,
and the moon's sly light
blurs his praying form;

there the luminous stars devise
a cunning halo,
(tall poplars semaphore
the coming storm);

and a storm flays his body,
spinning the world in
its fiery eye the storm
unravels the night –

whence (trousered, rheumatic,
increasingly mortal),
Jones returns to the vulgar
Bathed in Light.

The Laying of a Ghost

1

She curtsies to the roses
amongst which a naked stone man
on his pedestal poses
no questions. Begins to can-can,
hoiking her hem past her eyes
to bare to him but not witness – ,

    – no man alive,
frozen too on that terrace or
caught turning into that drive
can ask, nor can she answer;
she is, cunt bared to the sun,
until she drops her skirts to run.

2

All over the kitchen floor
a dried-out rain. Five even storms
of dust, defining steps. At
the breakfast-bar a warm chair.
I'm up in my boudoir, she calls,
with the dead, here are my wigs
and my new comb. She fingers
the dead white plastic grip in her hair.
I wish the wireless wouldn't talk
she says, as if I were there,
oh take me to the reservoir
where the sails of the boats are red;
oh kiss my eyes, my eyes, she says.

3

And when we take him to the terminus
his plane fails to arrive,
or crashes out of cloud at us,
burnt out, and he survives.

And so we go further,
the road blurs under our wheels
our rapt songs keel
across skies without murmur
night after night after night...

Stars hum their mechanical tunes;
'eyes white as marbled moons,
mouth black with lies,
I will curl up, beaten ball,
in my old cold heart and die.'

4

Always a mute snuffing wind
to set the loose door clicking.
I am always last to call.
She has sealed his eyes, has pinned
the note to his heart, pricking
it in with rose-thorns, that tells all;
Here lies the body of Grief,
Dementor of Minds, Heart-thief.

She smiles, 'it is almost time
to raise him, stone among roses,
and carve your indelicate rhyme.'
His right eye opens, closes.
Her hands, winding mine in silk,
white, inevitably, as milk.

Theirs

Because the stream was theirs, no-one listens;
it babbles on, we say, like any bore about his travels.
(Where their fledglings are baptised kingfishers swoop,
their own initiations long forgotten.) Yet
here their Mystic tore his heart and cried, 'This
is the natural habitat of love.' And lovingly

they wrote the stream's song down; its song
described the meeting of two wooded mountain-sides,
bird, deer and fox stooped to its rim.
Then drinking its silver flesh in
why do our minds not flood with clear hosannas?
It tastes of mud to us, dank stones, drowned wood, old tyres;

because the stream was theirs no-one listens.

At Langley

An express train shooting south
shot off the rails at Langley,
reared up out of its cutting
and charged the clock-tower down.

Took half the village with it
as it plunged down through the valley,
tore brick and iron and crying flesh,
smashed the glass-skinned reservoir and drowned.

We didn't go dredging for it. The fact
of huge disaster, the agonies
and heroics it generates, is fiction
here, Langley being one of those places

it couldn't happen. All's quiet
beyond our rain-smudged windows.
Sometimes a car glides by
with its load of deadmens' faces.

3rd World War Song

Battleships ride the swelling sea
and hook from it torn fishes
with guns patrol the purple sky
and pluck white feathers from it

orders belch from their officers' mouths
each captain's eye is starry
oh every landlocked mother knows
that battleships are holy

for skinny gulls and capsized whales
rock in the tide to prove it
when battleships dock to tears and cheers
and boys spill out of their turrets.

3rd World War Song

'How gently does the sun
set in your violent mind,
do my tendernesses calm
your burning blood?' He raised

his livid head, my son,
he raised appalled white eyes
and said 'how gently
must a man reply to guns?'

The sun set like a fire-
bomb in the suburbs, it
stained our quietly papered
walls flame-red. 'How grievous

shall my grief be, how
fiercely must I beg
to be revenged for this
when you are dead?' But stars

had multiplied like shrapnel
in his mind, like barbed-
wire snagged in the hearts
of humankind; he raised

a final finger, it
pumped blood like a gun,
he shot his tender brains out
my proud son.

The Recruits

1 Baptism of Thomas the Doubter

To rise, streaming love,
and run the green road home
– believer, exultant – and burst
in on their dumb, tanked lives –
his blowsy son, his boorish daughter
and nerve-wracking wife – and shout
I'll tread the road with Jesus! –
the one clear climax of his life.

2 Fishers of Men

I wonder what they told their wives about him,
what were their nagging doubts,
grouped there under the eucalyptus
gutting their glut of fish, steeling themselves
to leave with the miracle-worker.

Or whether they could picture him
shouting those innocent words
about being broken, being let down,
up there on his cross in the gruelling heat,
hurt to death by the nails,
begging my God don't let me die
like fishermen clawing their nets in during a storm.
And whether, if they could, they would have gone.

Glimpse, of a Girl I Can't Look At

Blinded, she listens for eyes –
that tell-tale click as they swivel,
the whistle of lashes –
to gauge what parts of her

they focus on. Some linger on
her breasts, and some her mouth; all
stop at the whites of her eyes.
All stop; not all survive;

those that stare too long,
or pityingly, her delicate fingers –
unerring as missiles –
strike out.

The stricken repeat their cries.
She hears them, she regrets, but
like the sighted crowd about her,
turns a blind eye.

Coillieghillie

If a porpoise
under the gleaming hoop
of its own back
in the rise and the fall

of a seaway
could with its air-vent
do more than breathe, could
vary its husky music

and make melody,
would it be
waltz-time? Pibroch? A shanty?
Coillieghillie

abandoned, half-saved,
with views to Skye
and the flat hat of Raasay,
on breathless evenings

when the sun's low glide
is about to complete
its exquisite chameleon
dyeing of the sea,

and oystercatchers' skrilling
and the stonechat's clirk
instinctively cease,
and our breath's stopped too, and

pssssh pssssh pssssh pssssh
porpoises are heard
before they're seen – and we
seem momentarily separate

as two stones – you
summon musings consequential
as these. And then the sky's lid
closes on the sea.

The Tip

Take this 5p,
round and clear-rimmed
as the false earth
astronauts see
from their billion-pound craft,

and bleep via satellite
home with such rash
human love.
A disc of pure delight?
Or alloyed conceit, forged

in the infinite above.
But take it; as if
love were wooing you life
might depend on your keeping
your distance from it,

but not letting go.
Look to the priceless void.
Study the stamped-on moon.
Beware the heady clink
of stars in your pockets.

Flood Alert

(fear of suffering a heart attack)

It feels like the whole sky dissolving
till all that is left is water
falling and soaking through clothing,
through skin, to hang in clot-like drops
from the roof of your heart.
The universe, it's failing –
you hear, in your nerved-up mind,
in the cloud-high brain above,

a drip, drip, drip,
as if somewhere, planets away,
something were bleeding. Or perhaps
it is only God's innocent waters
falling in drops from a tap?
Hearts stop, in spite of themselves.
The brain turns to rain,
each drop of it quaking, and hangs there

dismayed, dreaming up rainbows, an Ark.

Love and the Undertaker

Like doves of peace,
so flutteringly alive
in that candled dimness,
his hands ushered me out

after the viewing.
They were powder-white,
he resides in
chromed and marbled chambers,

creates out of sight.
They preen, they flutter
so beautifully! And touch
discreetly, deferentially

as the dearest callgirl's.
Oh dear, dear girl
your corpse and you were different
as waxdrops and tears,

I cried live tears
for your bridal-gowned limbs
and stopped eyes.
But those doves knew when

to fly, to stall, to light
on my shaking shoulders,
to whisper, to guide –
they feed on tears,

on tremulousness, lost lives.
Will I ever know such love again?
with what remains of you
he'll come calling tonight.

Suicide Pact

Shall I, she said, scream now or will you act?
She'd slit her wrists so often – and this is fact –
that the healed skin held no feeling. And what,
her bold eyes said, can you do about that?
Death without pain – the thought's beautiful
enough to turn minds giddy. She straddled the pool
of blood from that red-lipped gash in her arm
and laughed – not even death, she said, can do me harm.

If only she had screamed I would have acted,
but I stayed still. At last she reacted
by thrusting the mouth-like wound right under
my lips. What use are words, I wondered,
when flesh can be articulate as this?
And stooped to that first, intense, salt-frenzied kiss.

The Seduction

He opened his hands and loveliness flew up,
a winged image of what his feelings were.
It settled on the flowered rim of his cup
and turned its feelers questingly to her.
Her lashes dropped across her eyes like nets –
he formed the feeling she was poised to lunge
across the table, yet sat still. It's
plain he thought she thought he'd take the plunge.
Failing to note her eyes spring wide as jaws
he sent his fluttering hands to cup her breasts –
her mouth clamped round his mouth with such frank zest
he had to writhe away and force a pause.
And then she sprang, upsetting the tea-things,
and flew him round the room on nightmare wings.

Atishoo, Atishoo

All God's porpoises are
swooping down from the sun,
they're having a whale of a time,
such hooligan foolings around.

(But look at the holes they've blown
in our road – to whom should we complain?
Will the police not come round?)
And the fireworks – that lunatic

catherine wheel's a fright,
it's, look, cartwheeling round,
first melting down windows, now brickwork –
even the Clock Tower's down.

And what is that billowing cooling-tower –
constructed of smoke – see, there,
casting its delicate brand
of genetic mayhem down –

is it real? Or have films
on their silver spools unreeled
in the sky and all our silly brains
tuned in to nightmare?

O television oozing
our final sounds – peacemakers
pounding steel tables, ministers
going to ground – don't fade,

don't leave us nothing! The trees
on the street are torches,
our clothes flake apart. Let's
hold each other to each other's hearts

and feel how those porpoises leap,
dears, shimmying round and round,
looping loop after loop, till
we all fall down.

Dissection

Listen. Your poem has all but died
in its swamp of sound. We
can see it like your Adam's apple
gulp – there – just hear it
croak, frog-like, from the mud
of some silted-up river, aground
in your once-navigable mouth; but

there's nothing we can do to salvage it.
So let us peel the skin back,
let us spread the raw flesh
and demonstrate the heart of it still
fluttering, little, so pinkly
inadequate now it's bared. Don't wish
you'd never tried to utter it. You'll

feel – we do assure you – quite dead.

Champagne Corks

Wine leaps in the cup of my hands,
a comet's tail of froth shot from
the clean, the tinselled world of champagne
bottles. Stoop to it, love,
as superstition's vampires stoop to blood
lap it hungrily up till the cup
of my flesh is bare, replenished, bare;
then lie down in my arms on the dark earth's floor.

There flies the moon, tipped on his back,
his body bold as ours; and bats
are at their devilry under the trees. Is it not
a marvel that folk from our carnal world
can woosh like champagne corks up to the stars?
Imagine making this beast-with-two-backs on Mars!

Amateur Boxing

Two boys with leather cages strapped
to their heads are fighting to lift
big barbells, one in each hand. They
sway about, then drop them on
each other. Smoke squirms in the spot-

lit air, feet scuffle over
the drum-skin floor like brushes.
It's sore, and now one's stuck
to the fence, behind his arms,
and the other one's bouncing his

barbells on and off them. Everyone's
shouting, all the burly diners
in bowties and starch, and one
little monkey's in the square
with them, those boys whose heads loll

in cages, jibbering and crouching
and flagging his arm up and down.
All this in a chandeliered hall
with white plasterwork and puce curtains
and port-stained table cloths.

At last the boys give up and their
heads are let out. I'd sooner be
the monkey – he's small, but he's
hoisting one of their barbells above
his head no bother at all.

Anniversary

(for Wenna)

Some tunes never develop beyond a few bars.
Landlubbers launch expecting to navigate oceans.
It's sad when friends stop loving each other,
when passionate faces contort over lists of possessions
and feelings forced in the hot-house fug of marriage
are weighed in the frosty palms of solicitors.

Mulling you over – humming old themes, sounding new
depths –
I find no wicket-gate you've nudged me through has led
to that walled garden where nothing changes,
where I become wholly I and you are completely you –
that graveyard called Eden.
You taught me never to say forever, never

to petrify our lives in glaze; to be dis-satisfied,
restless as waves which come and come again and still crave
oceans.
Or is that what I taught you?
We're riding a mare with a sensitive mouth,
she's confident but twitchy, not wholly predictable;
we've a long, maybe a shortening way to go.

And it's twenty years since we started and I'm
madder now for your body, more in love with unfathomable
you,
and we've deserts to cross, and seas, apart, together.
Some nights our dreams go surfing out of control.
Two bodies shape one question-mark under our covers.
Another twenty years, best friend and lover?

Why Hast Thou Forsaken Me?

Whatever prayer is like it's not
ventriloquist lips intoning responses. Not
candle-white hands in the gloom, not
whispers jostling for room in the high roof-trusses.

But imagine that everything's over.
The lines are down and the coal-shed's empty.
Mice chew over the Word in abandoned churches.
Grass verges decline, unclipped.

And astronauts tuned to earth feel inter-
fered with. Their screens grow nervous tics.
They note 'atmospheric disturbance'
unexplained by astro-physics.

Tears and shrieks invade their dreams,
beggars, conmen and essayists entreat in their heads.
Then the earnest, the well-meant, wild mystics,
the priests and the prophets and even the risen dead –

yet Earth still shines like a new watch in their dark.
If those astronauts were us and our
booster-rockets were dud and mission-control
went dead and that seemed that, would we

mouth MAYDAY MAYDAY till our batteries were flat?
The man who spread his palms
to be nailed down thought he would fly.
His truest prayer was that oh so human cry

about love that lasts till it stops, like eggtimer sand;
about time that ticks till it's not.
It's riding downhill without brakes on your bike.
It's questions without answers. That's what prayer's like.

Thought-Beasts

Behind the pretty walls of her head
and its cute shut shutters, lies her mind.
Her mind steals out on the limb of itself
searching the darkness with octopus stealth –

and Giant Squid are said to have dragged
ships down, suckered men under the waves
till terror drowned them, water filled their chests,
and beaks sharp as marlinspikes bloodied their vests.

Her lashes drip distress. Why do the peace-
whales we cherish writhe in nets?
                    May her mind
lie like a billiard-ball, snug
in the pocket of her head. May calm adults

search the crannies of her room –
as divers might a sunk ship's hold,
stabbing their torch-beams at eye-glints –
and kill all thought-beasts dead.

Half Out of This World

A jet stands on its wingtip in the blue,
half out of this world, past music, applause
and the humbling scuffle of shoes. Tom
watches through a plate-glass window, blindly.
Someone shouts for nurse, nurse comes, and goes,
shifting beneath her uniform in Tom's
mind, part of some dumbshow too.
                                    The jet now
pirouettes beyond the focus of Tom's
glass lens, and only treetops ruffle its
square of blue. Someone shouts for nurse, nurse comes,
she holds Tom to the bottle while he pees
and trees flaunt their greenery through the glass.
Just off-screen an error of judgment
is hurling lumps of jet into the grass.

You, Turning the World Upsidedown

I used to believe
there was always a hill
beyond what we thought was the summit,
a road dotted with headlamps
snaking to it
and faces behind blind windscreens
craning up like flowers to gulp down light.

You made me pull into lay-bys
and sleep. Then woke me
to supple horizons
all sheer as earth's shivering dawn edge
and curved as your lashes,
your kissed lips, your hip's rim;
then took turns driving with me.

I'll love you until
they blast us into the ether
and earth's like a spec on that starmap
we pinned to our childrens' wall
and you say
God, such brilliance,
but shouldn't it be up the other way?

The Cloud Is Breaking Up

The cloud is breaking up. You can see through
to the blue umbrella of the sky.
You walk a few steps. The clouds close up
and you forget the sun's there too,
bright as the butt-ends that fly
in gay arcs from the parapet to the river.
You stamp your earth-bound boots and cup
white hands, eyeing the weather.

Over you, and cloud, and sun, in the universe's
far blue skin, a tear is widening –
your future peers through. You tip your purse
and scatter notes that promised nothing.
Elation fills you – you strip, and then
it bursts in. You jump clean out of your skin.

Lullaby

Move into sleep, now
moving, untouching,
hair, old quaint clothing
frail flags in the wind,
who touched, then
as breezes, the quick skin
of lovers, triggered the breath,
the dear bruising of love
then, move, now
untouching,
in sleep now
dear old one,
flags all in tatters,
long love come to grief;

flags all in tatters,
long love come to grief.

The Fruit and Veg Puzzle

Life is a jigsaw-puzzle.
Keep your onion-eyes peeled
for the missing piece. Yeah,
so how come
there's no lid with a picture to copy?
And no-one can see for blubbering?

And who'd invent it anyway,
some cabbage-eared boy-god juggling
behind the circus tent with stars?
Yeah? And we're
just another dim world he dropped,
inexorably breaking up into flung-

apart pieces, mis-shaping
in petrified motion like Dali clocks?
And Time's just
the steam off some vast pot-pourri,
and our earth's no more than a sprout
spiralling into the pot? Yeah,

some jigsaw. But at least this clod
of a deity dreamed up
SEX – if not for himself. Well,
speaking met-
aphysically he's not of our vegetable
world; no seedpods, no balls. Ah,

the earthy, ineffable pleasures
of fitting the sex bits together,
infinitessimally slowly gyrating,
anemone-
fleshed, landlocked, at sea, pulsing
slowly as acorns becoming trees.

And love? Love's... knowing the rooty hand
of that clown behind the big top
is outstretched, and the fantastic circus
is waiting
for its crowd. Is knowing when
apples drop to the star-stained floor

that pips will pop out. Yeah, some jigsaw.

The Revenge

"Hands always are the liveliest of features,
and the wrists that animate them – if they're slender –
whose veins translate the rhythms of the heart."
Your words, she smiled, you lovely blue-veined creature,
teasing his throat between one thumb and finger,
grazing his eyelids with her lips apart.
His hands twitched in their attitude of prayer –
though stretched above his head and cruelly tied –
as she briefed their weeping daughter. *"Prepare*
the blade and the bowl. Now, prise the mouth wide
and force this rubber bar between the teeth.
Good. And don't forget the severed arms will flop
unless propped by these braces from beneath."
The throat between her red nails shrieked and shrieked.

Sketch; from Back-of-Keppoch, Arisaig

White topmast seen over rocks;
Skye's blue, smudged hills.

Back sizzles like a hotplate in the sun.
Out on the blue-grey acres tan-and-white sails,

a bowsprit – white-tipped too – the flash
of her bow-wave cool as an icecream cone.

Your body creamy-cool too, and I
the tall-limbed cutter cleaving its ocean.

Macduff Times 3

1

From east of Macduff I saw west of Banff
a field's pelt blown to the clouds,
the brown of it brawling down cliffs and out

to sea. 4 miles off the fishers
netted a dustbowl, and the shy sun
hid her head in a fine-tilthed veil.

2

Make slits of your eyes.
Look at the scrambled-egg fields
above Macduff. Can such yellows be real?

As rape is. As unrequited love.
As drinking alone is.
As stone walls, Macduff.

3

In 'the hovel', Macduff,
3 men grinned and fluttered their paper poems.
Gulls on the slates exchanged ecstatic squeals.

Macduff is where I learnt
how boats are built the lost way,
and how exiles feel.

Irises

Margaret is 20 years dead.
The irises she painted in dense oils
have the dated look of velvet,
thick greens and mauves to be worn
by onlookers at a funeral.
They hang without breathing over his bed.

Emptied of blooms
the stone-white pot she fashioned
at evening classes – to keep
her fingers supple – looms   .
like a victorian jug, an urn
giving form to darkness. Which floods

my head – I can't stop seeing
eternally sharpened pencils;
that eyeless figurine
with wire joints you can twist –
for Art's sake – to excruciating poses;
corroding pages of sketches.

Who's dead? Stench dribbling
from a commode, that chrome-railed bed,
the toilet-roll tied to the TV stand;
each tells its story. When Jim
tries his, rubbing his flaky scalp
with fingers like penises, he can't remember.

David, You Beauty

after a friend told me she was moved to
tears by Michelangelo's David

We haven't met but
I know what you look like
naked. I'm glad
your mother was washing – her
Monday routine? – your
only dress. Thank Apollo
it wasn't hailing! And for

your immaculate musculature –
poor you might have been
(no sandals, no sunhat,
no shades) but
the diet was right. Or
is that a spot you're
scratching? And willy lying

there on your balls looks
I have to exclaim
so cute! Has he ever been
in the wars? I bet
yes, but hope that elastic waist
has never been forced
across the parallel bars

of pain, or those marble
buttocks prised unwillingly.
Are you soldier? Student? Rent-boy?
Do you know how
disturbing you are? Hey,
a friend of mine,
from a rawer climate than yours,

circa 1995 – that's
how ancient you are –
having seen the cream of
Italy's treasures – and she
with her lover –
met you and wept, wept for
your beauty. Boy, that's power.

Degas Undressed

A sketch

Let the old man out
of his bowler hat and the flying cloud
of his beard, watch him twirl

the many-coloured umbrella of his genius
in the air. Let him stand
naked as a woman bent to a chipped bowl

under the torrent of her hair
in an old buff's painting. Let him understand
the sagging of his belly and feel

the puny gristle of bared buttocks.
See how he wields his flannel in the tub
like an artist's rag of rainbows,

an artiste's boa – how amazed we are!
The lights are popping like fireworks, the old
man has become a blether of colour,

the audience sits dazed. Whispers
swarm amongst them and backstage dancers
are fluffing blue tutus for his finale.

Looking at the Apple

Ignoring Mr Newton the apple
reclaims its branch. Watch how its plumpness
shrinks until it flies tight as a golfball
at that greenhouse; see it explode through glass.
Hear trees suck back the sap from leaf to root
and relive their pasts. See me, in flannel
shorts, mouth hanging wide as I race
to the itching wood – up to my ankles
in needles, shrubs to my resinous knees –
of new-fangled firs. Laugh as old Mr Smith
the gardener bellows and stamps like Goliath,
a frost of splintered glass in his tattered hat.
Re-load those catapults with apple-shot.
Storm the ancient orchard and reclaim your fruit.

Natural Selection

(driving home after a poets' night out)

Look out there's
a poem smack
in the headlights – wow
near miss.

How many peeking
out, dashing
for it, get snared
by your brilliance?

Are most reduced
to stains – tyre-marked,
gut-splattered furs?
Call yourself poet?

So why in the name
of all that quivers
beyond the pencil-stab
of our lights

do you murder
them, beasts you claim
rapport with, various,
rabbit-shaped tonight?

Stop. Extinguish
the lights. Wait. See?
Silhouettes, free movement
naturally selected;

wild, and at ease.

Biographical Note

Ian Crockatt was born in 1949 in Perth, and lived in nearby Scone till he was eleven years old. He moved south to Merseyside with his family in 1960, and his secondary education was at a Quaker boarding school in York. This was followed by a year as a VSO, teaching at a secondary school in Western province, Kenya.

Three years in Birmingham resulted in an Eng Lit degree, marriage, and a handful of poems. Two more years of various jobs, including several months on a Kibbutz in Israel, led him back to Birmingham to take a Diploma in Social Work while Wenna, his wife, gained a diploma in Art and Design. Since then he has worked as a social worker in Dudley, Fort William, Devon and Grampian. At the moment he is a senior social worker in North Aberdeenshire, commuting on a weekly basis from his home by the Caledonian Canal in Bavanie, Fort William, where his wife's pottery is based. He and Wenna have been married for 26 years and have three teenage children.

A few of his early poems were published in 1976 by Outposts Publications in a booklet called *On Each White Page.*

Much of his spare time is spent in, or working on, small sailing boats.

Acknowledgements

Particular thanks to Alan Jamieson, Richard Crockatt, Pat Morrisey, Tom Bryan and Stuart Campbell who, at different times and in different ways, offered that blend of go-for-it and judicious criticism that makes the difference between developing as a writer and not writing for publication at all.

And to Wenna, for so much.